Published by:
Positive Press Ltd,
28A Gloucester Road,
Trowbridge,
Wiltshire
BA14 0AA

Telephone: 01225 719204. Fax: 01225 712187
E-mail: positivepress@jennymosley.co.uk
www.circle-time.co.uk

Text © 2017 Jenny Mosley
Illustrations by Mark Cripps and Clare Mortimer
Printed 2017
© 2017 Positive Press Limited

ISBN: 978-1-904866-90-9

Printed in the UK by www.heronpress.co.uk

Contents

Introduction

Hula hoop games provide the ideal opportunity to engage children in enjoyable activities together, promoting positive relationships between the children themselves as well as the children with the adults.

The games encourage valuable social skills such as:

- Turn-taking
- Developing speaking and listening skills
- Developing a positive attitude to participation
- Learning to abide by rules
- Interacting with others
- Co-operating
- Having fun

Hula hoop games also encourage physical exercise, which is important and often-neglected in today's hi-tech society and is an essential part of physical wellbeing.

The hula hoop games included in this booklet are set out in a clear, accessible style with easy-to-follow instructions. Hula hoop games provide an ideal occupation for free time that can motivate all children to be part of a group.

They will enhance playground experiences for the children involved, creating a positive dynamic and generating great fun and enjoyment for all.

Four Square Hoops

Number of players: Groups of four

What you need: Four hula hoops, four bean bags for each group

What you are learning: Balance, social skills, gross motor skills, coordination, motor control.

How to play:

Set up the hula hoops in the shape of a square on the ground, and have one bean bag in each hula hoop. The children will be in the press up position, with their hands behind their hula hoop.

When you say "Go" the children will try to toss their bean bag into one of the other three hula hoops belonging to the others in the group. The child trys to remove any bean bags that land in their hoop. To end the game call "Stop". The children will see how many bean bags they have in their hula hoop. Each bean bag represents a point. The object of the activity is to have the fewest amount of points at the end of each round.

To mix things up slightly, have the children start in different positions. For example: plank, standing, standing on one leg or kneeling them grow as a learners and as individuals.

Rabbit Hole

Number of players: Group

What you need: Hula hoops, cones or other objects to lift hoop off the ground.

What you are learning: Balance, social skills, gross motor skills, coordination, motor control.

How to play:

Balance the hula hoops on top of the cones to create a hole that they can step into. Tell the children that they are all rabbits, and they have to get into their rabbit hole to hide before the fox finds them.

Designate one child as the fox and have them chase the other children into the hole. The children must step over the hula hoop with each foot to arrive in the hole without knocking the hula hoop from the cones. If a child knocks the hula hoop down, they join the fox in the chase.

Continue the game until all of the rabbits have been caught!

Hula Hooped

Number of players: As many as you like in pairs or small groups.

What you need: Hula hoops, cones or other objects.

What you are learning: Hand-eye coordination, maths skills.

How to play:

For this game set out cones for the children to toss the hula hoops onto. The goal is to ring the hoop around one of the cones.

For an added interest add values to the cones for the children to add up their total number of points. The pair or group with the most points wins!

Snakes

Number of players: Group

What you need: Hula hoops

What you are learning: Team work

How to play:

This is a much loved hula hoop game for the whole class. The children hold hands to form a line or a circle. Choose a child to start the snake. The children must then pass the hoop down the line or around the circle, without letting go of one anothers hands, or allowing the hoop to touch the ground.

Wizard's Hoopla

Number of players: Group

What you need: Hula hoops, somewhere to hang the hoops, string, bats and balls

What you are learning: Hand-eye co-ordnination, maths

How to play:

Hang the hula hoops from a tree, or a goal post at varying heights. The children use bats and take it in turns to hit the balls through the hoops. To make the game more exciting add values to the hoops, and split the group into teams.

Alternatively to up the difficulty level create a moving target by making the hoops swing. The group with the most points wins!

Musical Circles

Number of players: Group

What you need: Hula hoops, music

What you are learning: Listening skills

How to play:

Lay out the hula hoops on the floor, one less than the number of children taking part. Whilst the music is playing ask the children to walk around all of the hoops in any direction that they choose. When the music stops they must jump into a hoop of their own. One child should not be in a hoop, and is therefore out. They can help the teacher spot the last child in the next round. This continues until there is just one child remaining.

Colour Corners

Number of players: Group

What you need: Different coloured hula hoops

What you are learning: Skills

How to play:

Choose four different coloured hula hoops and set them in the corners of the play space on the ground. For large groups you may need two or three of each colour.

Choose one child to be 'Chaser' and another child to be the 'Colour Caller'. The colour caller calls out the name of a coloured hoop, and all the children must run to get inside that colour hoop before the chaser tags them. If the chaser tags a child, that child must then remain frozen until all players have been tagged.

The last player to be tagged then becomes the new Chaser and the game begins again.

Rolling Race

Number of players: As many as you like in pairs or small groups

What you need: Different coloured hula hoops, tape measure, paper and pencils

What you are learning: Skills, measuring

How to play:

This game works well when played in small groups, but can work as pairs or large groups. The group take it in turns to roll their hula hoops along the ground until it comes to a stop.

The group then works together to measure the distance from the starting point to the hula hoop, and records the measurements on the paper. The child with the furthest distance wins, and the group with the largest collective distance wins.

Through the Hoop

Number of players: Group

What you need: Hula hoops, stopwatch

What you are learning: Skills

How to play:

Ask the children to form a line. Give the first child in the line a hula hoop to hold above their head. Each child must take the hoop over their head down to their feet and pass it on to the next child. This continues until the hoop has been passed along to the end of the line. The better they work as a team the more their time will improve.

Alternatively, split the group into two lines and compete against each other to get the hula hoop to the end of the line first.

Hula Cars

Number of players: Group

What you need: Hula hoops

What you are learning: Skills

How to play:

Each child is given a hula hoop which they hold around their body. Ask the children to move around the play space pretending to be cars, but without bumping into each other. Call out different actions for the children to perform.

For example 'Bumpy Road' the children skip, 'Flat Tyre' the children gallop. Other actions include 'Red Light' the children freeze, and 'Spin Out' the children hula hoop.

You can also call out different road types to alter the childrens speed, For example 'Motorway' the children run, 'Street' the children jog and 'School Zone' the children walk.

Sorting Game

Number of players: Group

What you need: Hula hoops lots of classroom objects

What you are learning: Organising, alphabet, numbers, team work

How to play:

Place some hula hoops on the ground. Assign a letter to the hoops using a piece of paper. The children need to find objects and place them in the hoop with the correct letter. For example and apple would go into the hoop assigned to the letter 'A'.

Alternatively you could have the hoops assigned to numbers instead of letters, and the children have to put the correct amount of objects into the hoops.

House of Hoops

Number of players: Teams

What you need: Hula hoops and balls

What you are learning: Team work

How to play:

Split the group into two teams. House of Hoops is like building a house of cards. The house will stand on its own, but the slightest touch will knock it down.

To build a house of hoops, you must place one hoop on the floor, using four hoops to sit inside it forming the sides, adding another one on top to hold them together. The teams must build one or two of these hoop houses on their side of the play area.

One ball per five players is used to knock down the other team's, house of hoops, whilst protecting their own house.

A point is awarded each time a house is knocked down, even if a player bumps into his or her own house.

Houses that are knocked down should be set up as quickly as possible so play can continue.

The game is separated by a centre line, which players cannot cross to retrieve a ball.

Builders and Bulldozers

Number of players: Teams

What you need: Hula hoops and bean bags

What you are learning: Team work

How to play:

Scatter the hula hoops all over the playing area. For every hula hoop, you'll need one bean bag. Place half of the bean bags inside the hula hoops, and half outside the hula hoops.

Divide the children into two teams. One team will be the 'Builders'. The builders will run around and try to put the bean bags inside the hula hoops. The other team will be the 'Bulldozers'. They will run around and try to put the bean bags outside the hula hoops.

To start the game say, "Go!" The teams run around either building (putting bean bags inside the hoops) or bulldozing (taking bean bags out of hoops). We always have the rule you can't guard a hoop. Play continues until you say, "Stop!" Have all the players put their hands on their heads. Count how many bean bags are inside the hoops, and how many are outside the hoops. If there are more bean bags inside the hoops, the builders win. If there are more bean bags outside the hoops, the bulldozers win.

Hula Hoop Challenge

Number of players: Group

What you need: Hula hoop for each child

What you are learning: Balance, social skills, gross motor skills, coordination, motor control.

How to play:

The Hula Hoop Challenge consists of different ways of spinning the hula hoop.

The first move is 'Classic Hooping'. Holding the hoop around their waist and spinning it around themselves whilst wiggling their hips. Try asking the children to a step forwards or backwards whist spinning the hoop.

Adapting the ' Classic Hooping' move to 'Kneeling Hooping' by trying the same move whilst on their knees. See if the children can rise to standing position without dropping the hoop.

Moving onto the arms, 'Arm Hooping' is the next move. Holding their arm out straight spinning the hoop around their wrist in small circles. See if they can switch to another arm without stopping

'Hula Hop' is a move when the hula hoop becomes a jump rope. Try this move backwards too.

'Knees Hula' is achieved by putting their knees together, holding the hoop at the back of their legs and then start it spinning and see if they can keep it going on their knees. Can the children start with 'Classic Hooping' and move

through to 'Knees Hula' without dropping
the hoop?

The last move is 'Hula Skip'. The children put
the hoop on their foot with one foot inside the
hoop and one foot outside the hoop. Try to
spin the hoop around their ankle while hoping
over it with the other foot.

Training & Resources

Book Jenny Mosley for training and conferencing

We deliver conference days and training for positive behaviour, training for self-esteem, training for teachers, training for MDSAs by holding open conferences and INSET in behaviour, INSET for primary schools, INSET for early years and lunchtimes training. Our open conference days are open to all.

Jenny's training and INSET days aim to cover key policies, inspire positive change, raise self-esteem, improve morale, help schools and settings function well and address non-curriculum areas.

Browse Training & Conferencing at www.circle-time.co.uk or call 01225 767157 or email circletime@jennymosley.co.uk

Resources

Resources can help your initiatives come to life. A poster on the wall can speak up for you when you are busy working in other areas. We have carefully designed resources especially for schools, all of which are displayed in our catalogue and on our website.

All resources can be ordered through Positive Press shop at www.circle-time.co.uk or call 01225 719204 for a full catalogue.